April 16, 2002

2.8
0.5

George Shannon

LIZARD'S HOME

Illustrated by
Jose Aruego
and **Ariane Dewey**

Greenwillow Books New York

Watercolor paints and a black pen were used for the full-color art.
The text type is Kabel Medium.

Text copyright © 1999 by George Shannon
Illustrations copyright © 1999 by Jose Aruego and Ariane Dewey
All rights reserved. No part of this book may be reproduced or utilized in any
form or by any means, electronic or mechanical, including photocopying, recording,
or by any information storage and retrieval system, without permission in writing
from the Publisher, Greenwillow Books, a division of William Morrow & Company, Inc.,
1350 Avenue of the Americas, New York, NY 10019.
www.williammorrow.com

Printed in Singapore by Tien Wah Press
First Edition
10 9 8 7 6 5 4 3 2 1

Library of Congress Cataloging-in-Publication Data
Shannon, George.
Lizard's Home / by George Shannon; pictures by Jose Aruego and Ariane Dewey.
p.   cm.
Summary: When Snake starts sleeping on the rock where Lizard lives, Lizard must figure
out how to get his home back.
ISBN 0-688-16002-6 (trade).   ISBN 0-688-16003-4 (lib. bdg.)
1. Lizards-Fiction.   2. Snakes—Fiction.   I. Aruego, Jose, ill.   II. Dewey, Ariane, ill.
III. Title.   PZ7.S5287Lh   1999   [E]—dc21   98-41055   CIP   AC

For Susan, as she sings *her* home
—G. S.

For Susan, Ava, and Phyllis
—J. A. and A. D

Lizard sang as he walked toward home after playing all day with Toad.

"Zoli zoli zoli—zoli zoli zoli.
Rock is my home—rock is my home.
Zoli zoli zoli..."

A few more feet, and he'd curl up snug on his rock to sleep.

But when Lizard got home,
Snake was sound asleep on his rock.

"Hello?" Lizard cleared his throat. "I'm afraid you've made a mistake. Everybody knows *this* rock is my home."

"SSSSSSsssssss," said Snake. "*I* don't make mistakes. I found it. I'll keep it. It suits me fine."

Lizard ran to ask Toad for help.

"Not me!" Toad gulped. "She could swallow us whole."

That night Lizard sat at a distance, watching Snake snore.
It had been Lizard's rock since the day he hatched.
Now he didn't have a place to go. As the locusts chirped,
Lizard sang a wish song to help him fall asleep.

"Twink a little, blink a little,
High up in the sky, a little.
Rock a little, hope a little,
Hope, and snake will go..."

When Lizard woke the next morning, Snake was gone!

Lizard ran to tell Toad that his wish had come true.

But when he got home, Snake was sitting on his rock again.
Lizard took a deep breath. "Perhaps," he said,
"you've mistaken my rock for another one.
Everybody knows *this* rock is my home."
"SSSSSSsssssss," said Snake. "I don't make mistakes.
I found it. I'll keep it. It suits me fine."

Snake hissed again, and Lizard ran to hide
among the pebbles and burrs.
As the stars came out, Snake began to snore.
But Lizard was determined not to fall asleep.
He'd reclaim his rock as soon as Snake left to eat.
To help stay awake, he sang his wish song fast:

> "Twink a little, blink a little,
> High up in the sky, a little.
> Rock a little, hope a little,
> Hope, and Snake will go…"

He sang faster, then slower. Then he sang *and* danced.
But by the middle of the night he was snoring, too.

Lizard woke at dawn and slowly opened one sleepy eye.
Snake was gone!

In a leap Lizard was home on his rock
and grinning as he went back to sleep.

He was still asleep when the sun went down.
"SSSSSSssssss," said Snake. "GET OFF MY ROCK!"

Lizard jumped awake. He knew just singing a wish wouldn't work this time. He took a deep breath and said, "*I* found it. *I'll* keep it. Everybody knows it suits *me* fine."

"I FOUND IT," said Snake. "And everybody knows *I* don't make mistakes."

"Please be fair," Lizard begged. "At least give me one chance."

"No."

Lizard shook his head. "But everybody knows that not being fair is a big mistake."

"I never make mistakes," said Snake.

"All right. You get one chance."

"Great!" said Lizard. "We'll get a sack with two pebbles—
one black, one white. If I grab the black, I get to stay.
If I grab the white, you get to stay. And I'll never say
you made a mistake again."
"Okay," said Snake with a shifty grin. "But I get to choose
the pebbles and sack."

"Fair enough," said Lizard. "I'll invite everyone
and meet you by the river when the sun comes up."

All his friends were at the river when Lizard arrived.
"Run!" said Toad. "You've got to hide. Rabbit heard Snake brag
that both pebbles she put in the sack are white. You'll lose
no matter which one you choose."

"Don't worry," said Lizard. "Everybody knows
Snake never makes mistakes."
He quietly sang as Toad shook his head:

"Twink a little, blink a little,
High up in the sky, a little.
Rock a little, hope—"

"QUIET!" said Snake. "Just close your eyes and reach in the sack. Black, you stay, just like you said. White, *I* stay."

Lizard slowly put his foot in the sack. Felt both pebbles.
Took one and yanked it out. But before anyone could see
if it was black or white, the pebble slipped loose
and sank in the river with a splash.

Snake laughed. "There's no way to prove what pebble you grabbed. You lost your chance!"

"No, I didn't," said Lizard with a snake-size grin. "There's still one pebble in the sack. If it's black, then mine was white, and you get the rock. If it's white, then mine was black, and *I* get the rock." Snake stammered, "But you can't be sure."
"Of course we can," said Lizard. "Everybody knows you don't make mistakes. I'm sure you fixed the sack and pebbles just right."

Snake slowly turned the sack upside down.
A white pebble fell out.

"Proof!" yelled Toad. "Lizard's *had* to be the black!"

"Proof!" Lizard grinned. "Rock is *my* home."

Everyone cheered. Lizard felt so good he couldn't help but sing all the way back home:

"Twink a little, blink a little,
High up in the sky, a little.
Zoli zoli zoli zoli.
Rock is my home!"